HOW TO IMPROVE AT MAKING
JEWELRY

YO-BCU-993

Sue McMillan

 Crabtree Publishing Company

www.crabtreebooks.com

Author: Sue McMillan
Editor: Adrianna Morganelli
Editorial director: Kathy Middleton
Prepress technician: Margaret Amy Salter
Production coordinator: Margaret Amy Salter

Photo credits:
Corbis: Bettman: page 6 (top); Randy Faris: page 47 (middle); Mimmo Jodice: page 5 (top)
Fotosearch: front cover, page 5 (bottom)

Getty Images: page 4 (bottom)
iStock: page 3 (bottom), page 7 (top), page 8 (all), page 9 (middle), page 9 (bottom), page 24 (bottom)
Photolibrary.com: page 5 (middle), page 6 (bottom)
Shutterstock: title page, page 7 (middle left), page 7 (middle right), page 7 (bottom), page 9 (top), page 47 (top), page 47 (bottom)
University of Bergen/Uni Global: page 4 (top)
All other photographs copyright © Search Press Ltd.

Library and Archives Canada Cataloguing in Publication

McMillan, Sue, 1973-
    How to improve at making jewelry / Sue McMillan.

(How to improve at--)
Includes index.
ISBN 978-0-7787-3577-9 (bound).--ISBN 978-0-7787-3599-1 (pbk.)

    1. Jewelry making--Juvenile literature.
I. Title. II. Series: How to improve at--

TT212.M34 2010   j739.27   C2009-907053-7

Library of Congress Cataloging-in-Publication Data

McMillan, Sue, 1973-
  How to improve at making jewelry / Sue McMillan.
    p. cm. -- (How to improve at...)
  Includes index.
  ISBN 978-0-7787-3599-1 (pbk. : alk. paper) -- ISBN 978-0-7787-3577-9
(reinforced library binding : alk. paper)
  1. Jewelry making. I. Title. II. Series.

TT212.M43 2010
739.27--dc22
                                        2009049080

Crabtree Publishing Company

www.crabtreebooks.com   1-800-387-7650

Published in Canada
Crabtree Publishing
616 Welland Ave.
St. Catharines, Ontario
L2M 5V6

Published in the United States
Crabtree Publishing
PMB 59051
350 Fifth Avenue, 59th Floor
New York, New York 10118

Printed in the U.S.A./012010/BG20091216

CONTENTS

INTRODUCTION

Since prehistoric times, humans have worn jewelry to decorate their bodies, ward off evil spirits, or to show people that they held an important position or belonged to a group. Bead jewelry has been worn by people for tens of thousands of years; the earliest examples of this kind of jewelry were made from snail shells.

GETTING CREATIVE

The wonderful thing about jewelry making is that, once you have learned the basic techniques, there is no limit to the pieces you can design. There are so many styles and materials that you can really let your imagination go wild!

You need some basic tools and materials. But if you are on a limited budget, you can keep costs down by hunting for old jewelry in secondhand shops. You will find that you can reuse many of the pieces, such as beads and fasteners.

GUIDE TO STEPS

In this book, we will show you step-by-step how to make many different pieces, including necklaces, bracelets, and earrings, using a variety of materials.

The process is broken down into manageable steps showing you the most important techniques for making pieces, from attaching clasps to making your own beads. Once you have mastered these examples, you can use your new skills to design fabulous pieces of unique jewelry!

A HISTORY OF JEWELRY

Jewelry has a long and varied history. The oldest forms were necklaces, probably made 75,000 years ago with snail shell beads. Other prehistoric necklaces and bracelets were made with bone, teeth, and stones. Later, jewelry makers created imaginative pieces with gemstones or precious metals. Today, all the materials of the past, as well as many new ones only recently available, are used in jewelry.

PREHISTORY

In Africa jewelry has been discovered that dates from the Stone Age. These simple snail shells were found in South Africa. The shells have holes in them as well as traces of **ocher pigment**, which suggests that they were once strung together as necklaces. The ocher was either used to decorate the shell or rubbed off from the skin of the wearer.

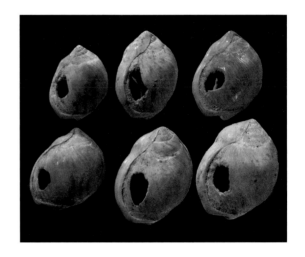

ANCIENT EGYPT

By the time of the ancient Egyptians, 3,000 years ago, jewelry making was an established craft. The Egyptians used a lot of gold, colored glass, and semiprecious stones, such as lapis lazuli and turquoise. Different colors and stones had different meanings. As well as being used to convey wealth and status, many pieces of Egyptian jewelry had **symbols** that were thought to protect the wearer.

ANCIENT GREECE

In ancient Greece, jewelry was also made from gold, semiprecious stones, and glass. The type of jewelry that the Greeks are most well-known for creating is the portrait **cameo** (right). Greek jewelry was mostly simple and was worn for special occasions rather than used every day.

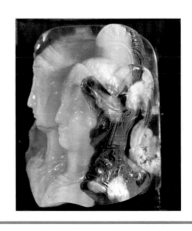

THE ROMAN EMPIRE

The ancient Romans were very fond of jewelry. The most common article was the fibula, or brooch, which was used to pin clothing. Roman jewelry was made from a variety of metals and was highly decorated with precious and semiprecious stones. Wealthy Roman women wore necklaces (left), bracelets, earrings, rings, and hairpins. Men usually wore only one ring.

CELTIC DESIGN

In the centuries after the Roman Empire, many cultures continued to create stunning pieces of jewelry. The Celts created **abstract** designs and wore torques (right), twisted metal collars or armbands, used to protect the wearer. In medieval times, only the wealthiest were permitted to wear gold and silver. Many pieces showed religious scenes painted with **enamels**.

DESIGN AND CHANGE

From the 1600s on, the advance in cutting techniques meant that gems, especially diamonds, could be used in many pieces in a wide variety of different styles. By the 1800s, floral motifs, or themes, were popular. Then the **Art Deco** movement took over in the 1930s, and jewelers began to create **geometric** pieces featuring a mixture of many gemstones.

INTO THE FUTURE

Modern jewelry uses many different materials, from traditional metals and gemstones, to beads, plastic, and glass. Jewelry is seen by many as wearable art, and some use it to identify with a particular group. Many people have started to make their own jewelry.

JEWELRY AROUND THE WORLD

Most pieces of jewelry are of value only to the wearer and do not cost a lot. But some pieces have become famous because they are so expensive or very beautiful. Some of these have an amazing story behind them. Others are well known because they are perfect examples of jewelry making as an art.

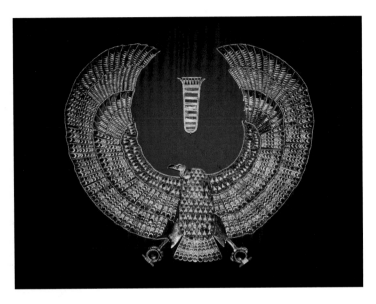

TUTANKHAMUN

More than 150 intricate pieces of jewelry were discovered in the tomb of the pharaoh Tutankhamun. Many are the finest examples of ancient Egyptian jewelry found to date. This vulture pectoral, or collar, was around the neck of Tutankhamun's mummy.

LALIQUE

René Lalique (1860–1945) produced some of the finest pieces of **Art Nouveau** jewelry. His pieces are prized by collectors for their beautiful design and craftsmanship. The moonstones and opals in this dragonfly decoration give it a shimmering quality.

FABERGÉ

When Carl Fabergé (1846–1920) is mentioned, most people think of the jeweled eggs that he created for the Russian tsars. However, he also created many stunning pieces of jewelry, including a famous diamond tiara which sold for over $1.6 million at auction recently.

Globally, there is a huge range of styles of jewelry, as well as a great variety of materials used. The reasons for adorning the body tend to be universal. However, different countries and societies create their own "looks."

AFRICA

In Africa jewelry has been made from all sorts of materials, including metals, seeds, and bone. Possibly the most striking pieces are the intricate beaded patterns worn by the Masai tribe (left) during special occasions such as weddings.

KAYAN NECK RINGS

In Myanmar, or Burma, women of the Kayan tribe traditionally wear brass neck rings. These rings are added gradually over years. They push down the collarbone, extending the length of the neck. No one is sure how this unusual and extreme custom started.

INDIA & INDONESIA

India has a long tradition of jewelry making, particularly with gold. Traditionally, Hindu women have to wear sixteen pieces of jewelry, including necklaces, bindi (a forehead decoration), and bangles. In Indonesia silver is a very popular metal for jewelry.

NATIVE NORTH AMERICANS

Native North Americans have a long tradition of using horn, bone, beads, feathers, and leather to produce striking pieces of jewelry of many kinds.

SYMBOLISM

Throughout history, some jewelry has had symbolic meaning. Probably the most well-known is the wedding ring, traditionally worn on the third finger of the left hand. It was thought that the veins in this finger led directly to the heart.

MEMBERSHIP

Some pieces of jewelry identify the wearer as belonging to a group. Probably the most common of these are the ones that represent religion. Some Christians, for example, wear a crucifix to show their faith, while Jewish people sometimes wear the Star of David. Many Catholics also carry rosary beads, a string of beads used in prayer.

COMMITMENT

In some cultures, an engagement ring is given before marriage to the woman to show that a couple are betrothed. In Ireland, Claddagh rings are given as a token of love.

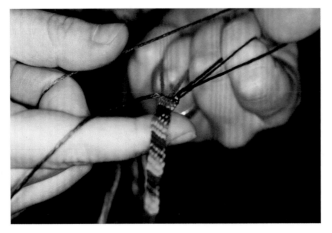

FRIENDSHIP

Some bracelets are made using embroidery thread. They are often exchanged as a sign of friendship. Traditionally the bracelet should be worn until it wears out or falls off.

CHARM BRACELETS

Charm bracelets are simple chain bracelets to which charms can be added. Usually a wearer will choose charms that have a personal meaning. Often they are added to symbolize important events in a person's life, such as the birth of a baby.

STATUS

Some items of jewelry are worn to show status. Throughout history, kings and queens have worn gold and jewels to show their position as the richest and most powerful people in their country. Queen Elizabeth I of England is shown here wearing lots of jewels. Gold chains of office are worn by some officials, including mayors, as symbols of power and authority.

PROTECTION

In many cultures, jewelry is worn to protect the wearer from evil. In parts of the Middle East and Mediterranean, charms with an eye symbol were used to ward off the bad luck from the "evil eye"—a bad look or a stare from someone. In some places, the evil eye charm is still worn today.

BEADS

Bead **threading** is one of the oldest and most straightforward forms of jewelry making. Today beads come in a dazzling array of materials including glass, plastic, clay, and metal, and are available in every color of the rainbow.

TYPES OF BEAD

BOHEMIAN GLASS—Almost limitless in range, these include round, **faceted**, and **fire-polished** designs that come in many different shapes, including hearts, stars, and flowers.

BUGLE—These long, tube-shaped beads are available in lengths.

CERAMIC—Use these beads to add **contrast** because they usually have a matt, or dull, appearance, not a glossy one.

CUBE—These square-shaped beads can be used to add extra interest to designs.

MAGATAMA DROPS—These beads have a large hole and are very useful for adding **texture** and **depth** to designs.

METAL—These small **spacer beads**, usually silver or gold, are great for adding some sparkle to your design.

SEED—These small, glass beads have a central hole and are sometimes called "rocailles."

SHELL PENDANTS

Pendants, or hanging ornaments, made from natural materials, such as these shells, make eye-catching focal points for your pieces of jewelry. Their variation in color and pattern will allow you to make truly unique pieces.

TOP TIP

Check the ends of bugle beads. Discard any that are sharp or cracked since they may cut the thread.

STORAGE

There are many ways to store your beads. The most convenient is in storage boxes (below right) that have separate compartments so that the beads can be sorted by type and color. While working, triangular dishes (below left) will help you to organize what you need.

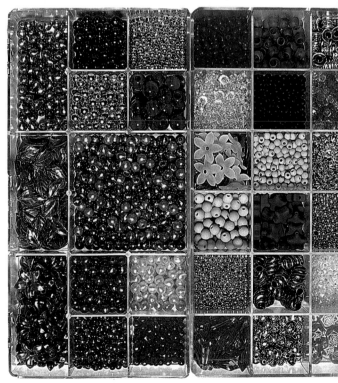

EQUIPMENT AND OTHER TOOLS

To make bead jewelry, there are a number of basic tools that you need. Some you will already have around the home. Others can be found at craft shops or online from specialty suppliers.

WIRE—There are many different types of wire available. You can choose by color, gauge (thickness), and strength. For designs that need to hold their shape, choose a lower gauge. If you need a flexible, delicate look, choose a higher gauge.

ACRYLIC PAINTS—For projects in which you want to paint jewelry, acrylic paints and a natural sponge, sponge brush, or bristle brush are essential.

RIBBONS, WIRES, AND THREAD—A number of different materials can be used. Collect ribbons, cords, braids, elastic, and fishing line, so that you can experiment with different finishes. Shells are also useful, if you can find them.

A MEASURING TAPE AND RULER—These are useful for checking thread, cord, and ribbon lengths.

GLUE—Adhesives, such as silicone glue, are used to attach items to your jewelry. A toothpick can be used to accurately place tiny drops of glue.

WOODEN SPOON—This everyday item can be used to twist wire.

SCISSORS—Scissors are essential for cutting thread, wire, and ribbon.

PLIERS AND WIRE CUTTERS—Two pairs of jeweler's pliers—one long-nosed, the other round-nosed—and a pair of wire cutters are essential pieces of equipment for jewelry making.

A KEEN EYE

Keep any attractive pieces of cord, ribbon, or thread you find, as they may be just the thing for a really eye-catching piece!

NEEDLES, THREAD, AND FINDINGS

As well as your essential tools, there are a number of small yet vital pieces of equipment that you will need in order to start your first jewelry project. These include needles and clasps, as well as many different types of pins.

NEEDLES

Beading needles are available in many lengths, the most common being about two inches (5 cm) long. The eye on beading needles is tiny, and this can make threading them a bit of a challenge. However, the smaller size allows the needle to pass through even the smallest of beads.

JEWELRY CABLE

This soft, flexible type of wire is ideal for projects in which you need to thread beads onto a straight wire.

THREADS, CORDS, AND CABLES

As well as wire, there are many different materials that you can use to thread beads. Nylon beading thread does not twist, so your beads will hang nicely. This type of thread is available in a number of thicknesses. If you want to use larger beads or need firm tension, use a thicker thread.

CLEAR ELASTIC CORD

This is ideal for using with any color of bead because it is transparent. It also has the advantage that it does not fray.

FINDINGS

"Findings" are the smaller pieces, such as rings and clasps, that you will need to create beaded jewelry. On this page are some of the different types you will need for the projects in this book.

1. FILIGREE BELL CAPS—These can be threaded on either side of a large glass bead to decorate it.

2. SPLIT RING—This is a double ring of wire, a bit like a very tiny key ring. It is ideal for using with a lobster clasp at the end of a bracelet or necklace.

3. JUMP RINGS—Made from a single loop of wire, these are used to attach pendants to a necklace.

4. CRIMP TUBES—Crimp tubes and crimp beads are used with jewelry cable to finish the end of the necklace. The tube or bead is squashed in place using a pair of pliers. Tubes are easier to work with than beads.

5. LOBSTER CLASPS—Used with split rings to fasten necklaces or bracelets, these are some of the most easy-to-use clasps.

6. MAGNETIC CLASPS—These clasps pull together because of the magnets inside. They are ideal for people who find clasps difficult to fasten. Magnetic clasps should not be used on jewelry if the person who will be the wearer has a pacemaker.

7. HEADPINS—These long pins with a head on one end can be used to make charms.

8. SAFETY PINS—These are very easy to use for different projects. Try threading beads onto the safety pins, then linking them to make interesting pieces. You can buy safety pins in many different sizes. As well as gold and silver, safety pins come in a variety of fun colors, including purple, green, and blue.

STRINGING AND PREP

There are a number of basic techniques used in beading. Once you have practiced and mastered them, you will be able to undertake a wider variety of beading projects to create exciting and imaginative pieces.

Before you begin any beadwork, prepare the thread by pulling it through a beeswax block, or thread conditioner, twice. This will stop the thread from fraying or tangling.

Picking up beads is trickier than it looks, so it is worth spending some time practicing. Here are a couple of tips:

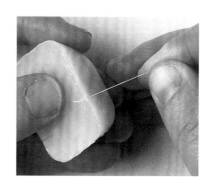

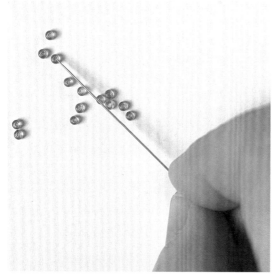

STEP 1

Put some of the beads on a flat surface. Place the end of the needle on the side of the bead you want to pick up. It is easier if you hold the needle at the end, as shown here. Take care to keep it as close to the work surface as possible.

STEP 2

Press down gently on the side of the bead, then flick it onto the needle, as shown. Do not worry if it takes a few tries to get this right. It will soon become second nature!

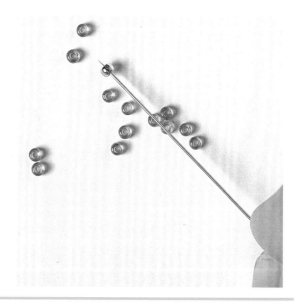

BASIC STRINGING

The easiest stringing technique is threading beads onto a length of thread. This is the oldest form of beading and the most basic technique that you have to master.

In order to create a string, it is important to use a tape measure to check how long it needs to be—in this case for a necklace. Once you are happy with the length, you can use the measurement to plan your design, spacing out the beads as shown.

STOPPER BEADS

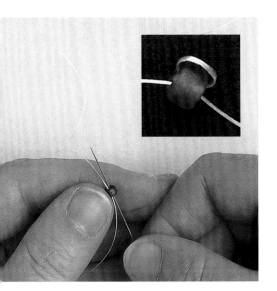

To start a string, you first need to make a "stopper bead" to prevent the beads from falling off the end of the thread. First thread your needle, then take a seed bead and pass the needle through it. Now repeat this step to create a loop around the bead as shown (inset left). There is no need to knot the thread. Make sure that you leave at least four inches (10 cm) of thread below the stopper bead.

PEYOTE STITCH

Peyote stitch is a beading technique used by many cultures, including Native North Americans who often used it to decorate ceremonial items. It is a beading technique in which beads are stitched together either as flat, long strips; round shapes; or tubes. The technique can be used to make jewelry, pouches, or to decorate items such as belts and ornaments. There are many types of peyote stitch; the most basic is called "even count."

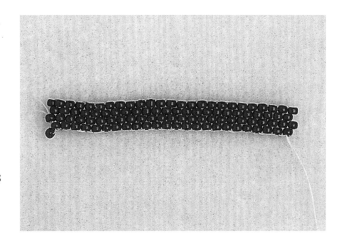

LINKS AND WIREWORK

In addition to being used for threading, wire is also handy for creating the links, clasps, and hooks that you will need for your creations. It can also be used to make whole pieces of jewelry with just a few beads added for decoration.

FLOWER LINKS
STEP 1

For these, use 18-gauge black wire. Take a length of wire three inches (7.5 cm) long, and create a loop by twisting one of the ends around a pair of round-nosed pliers.

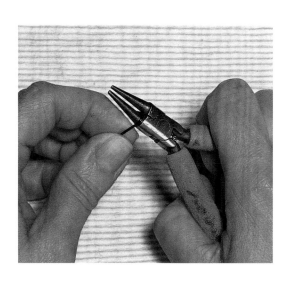

STEP 2

Make a second loop opposite the first. Now put the jaw of the pliers into the first loop, and make a third loop between the first two. Move the other jaw of the pliers into the first loop and wrap the wire again to make the fourth and final loop.

STEP 3

Use your wire cutter to trim off excess wire and finish your first flower link.

When working with wire, always wear safety goggles to protect your eyes from small pieces that may fly off when the wire is cut.

BEADED LINK
STEP 1

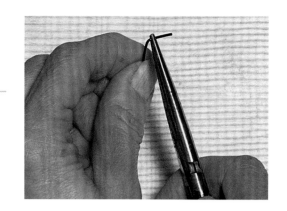

These can be used to join flower links. First, cut a one-inch (2.5 cm) length of wire and bend it at right angles about one-third of an inch (9mm) from the end using long-nosed pliers.

STEP 2

Now take the round-nosed pliers and roll the wire around the jaw to make a loop. Thread on a bead and then make a second loop in the same way.

HOOK CLASP
STEP 1

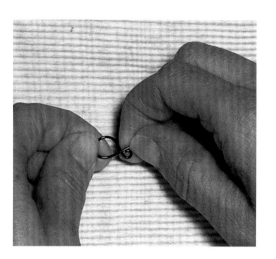

To make a clasp, cut a 1.75 inch (4.5 cm) length of wire. Make a simple loop at one end using round-nosed pliers. Now use your thumb to curve the other end of the wire around in a large loop, so that the end comes back on the small loop.

STEP 2

Use round-nosed pliers to curl in the end of the larger loop so that it forms a spiral.

All of these techniques can be used in a variety of ways. To make necklaces, earrings, or bracelets, join the bead links and flower links together. Use a hook clasp at each end to form the closing.

ETHNIC PENDANT

The necklace is probably one of the most common items of jewelry. This attractive pendant in natural colors is a great first project, and stringing beads onto jewelry cable is quick and easy.

You will need:
- 1 shell pendant
- 60 inches (1.5 m) jewelry cable
- 96 x 4mm bronze beads
- 30 ceramic beads
- 2 silver crimp tubes
- 1 silver lobster clasp
- 1 x 7mm jump ring
- 1 x 5mm split ring
- chain-nosed pliers
- cable snips or old scissors

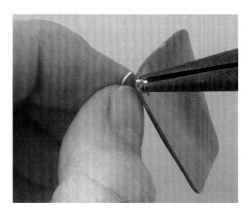

STEP 1

Open the jump ring with the cable-nosed pliers. Bend the ring slightly and place it in the hole in the pendant, closing it again with the pliers.

STEP 2

Take a length of jewelry cable. Use the end to pick up a silver crimp tube, followed by a lobster clasp. Bend the cable end and thread it back through the crimp tube.

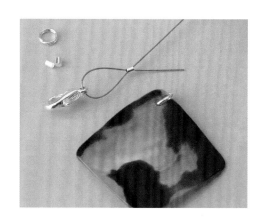

STEP 3

Use the chain–nosed pliers to squash the crimp tube flat. This will secure the clasp at the end of the necklace.

STEP 4

Using the cable snips or scissors, trim the tail of the jewelry cable beyond the crimping tube so that only one-half inch (1.25 cm) remains.

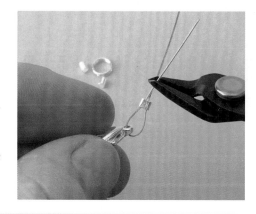

STEP 5

Now start threading the beads. Tuck the remaining one-half inch (1.25 cm) of the tail into the first three bronze beads, then thread on a ceramic bead and three more bronze beads.

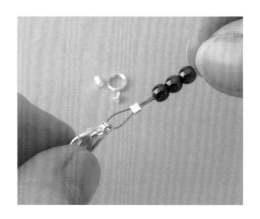

STEP 6

Continue this pattern until you have threaded 15 ceramic beads and 16 sets of bronze beads, as shown. Now thread the pendant and continue with the bead pattern, starting with another set of three bronze beads.

STEP 7

Once all the beads have been threaded, add the remaining crimp tube. Then thread the wire through the split ring, and loop it back through the crimp ring and two seed beads.

STEP 8

Pull the cable tight so that the loops at the end of the necklace are the same size. Then use chain-nosed pliers to squash the crimp tube. Finish by trimming the excess cable close to the bead. Now your necklace is ready to wear!

ETHNIC PENDANT

BUGLE NECKLACE

Now that you have made a single-strand necklace, try a triple-strand project. The bright pinks and purples work really well with the clear glass to make a really attractive piece.

You will need:
- 135 x size 11 pink seed beads
- 86 purple 6mm bugle beads
- 42 x 4mm round, clear glass beads
- 15 x 6mm round, clear glass beads
- 6.5 feet (2 m) lilac B beading thread
- 1 magnetic clasp
- beading needle
- sharp scissors

STEP 1

Thread the needle with the thread, pick up five pink seed beads, the magnetic clasp, then five more pink seed beads. Push the beads and clasp down the thread to leave a six-inch (15.25 cm) tail.

STEP 2

Loop the thread, as shown, left over right, then pass the needle through the loop to make a knot. Now make a second knot, passing the thread right over left.

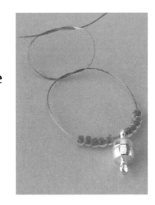

STEP 3

Pull the knot tight to make a ring of pink beads. Now use your needle to pick up the beads in this order: pink seed bead, purple bugle bead, pink seed bead, 6mm glass bead, pink seed bead, purple bugle bead, pink seed bead, and 4mm glass bead.

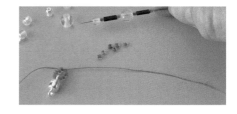

STEP 4

Repeat this pattern until you have threaded 15 x 6mm glass beads. Now pick up: pink seed bead, purple bugle, and pink seed bead. Next pick up five pink seed beads and put the needle through the free end of the clasp.

STEP 5

Pick up another five pink seed beads. Pull the thread through, then stitch back through the five pink seed beads, the clasp, and the five pink seed beads from step 4.

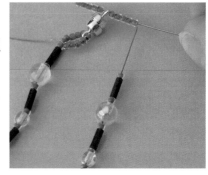

STEP 6

Stitch back through a pink seed bead, purple bugle bead, pink seed bead, 6mm glass bead, and a pink seed bead.

STEP 7

Now you add new beads by stitching through some of the first string. With your needle, pick up a purple bugle, a pink, a 4mm glass bead, a pink, and a bugle. Now stitch back around the necklace, picking up a pink, a 6mm glass bead, and another pink bead.

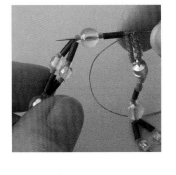

STEP 8

Repeat this along the length of the necklace until you come out of the last 6mm glass bead and stitch through a pink, a bugle, and a pink.

STEP 9

Stitch through the five pink beads at the end, the clasp, and the five pink beads at the other end. Go back through a pink, a bugle, 6mm glass bead, and a pink.

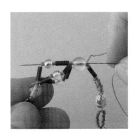

STEP 10

Pick up: bugle, pink, 4mm glass bead, pink, bugle. Stitch through a pink, a 6mm glass, and a pink. Repeat this pattern to the last 6mm glass bead, then stitch through a pink, bugle, pink. Now repeat step 9.

STEP 11

Make a loop passing the needle under the thread, and stitch through the loop to knot. Hide the end of the thread by stitching through one inch (2.5 cm) of beads. Snip the end, then repeat with the tail at the beginning of the necklace.

GLASS PENDANTS

Glass pendants are fascinating. They are created by firing, or heating, colored glass with metal oxides, and each piece is unique. These simple, elegant pendants are very easy to make.

You will need:

- glass pendant
- 20 inches (51 cm) faux suede ribbon (in two colors if preferred)
- 2 flat leather crimps
- 2 jump rings
- lobster clasp
- flat-nosed pliers
- sharp scissors

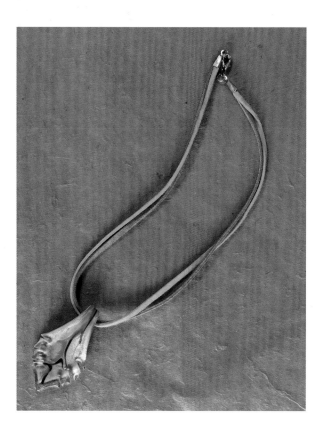

STEP 1

Figure out the length of the necklace, then cut the pieces of ribbon to this length.

STEP 2

Thread both lengths of ribbon through the pendant.

The island of Murano, in Venice, Italy, produces some of the world's finest glasswork. It is best-known for its multicolored glass called **millefiori,** *which means "thousands of flowers."*

STEP 3

Fix the flat leather crimps to the ends of the ribbons, making sure both lengths are held in place.

STEP 4

Use pliers to attach a jump ring to each of the crimps, then attach a lobster clasp to one of the jump rings.

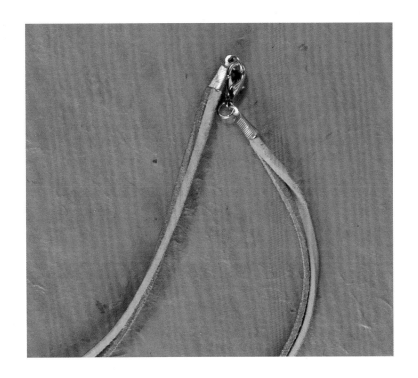

Colors

Use different color ribbons to add an interesting contrast or to bring out two shades in the pendant. Here, beige and turquoise have been used.

PENDANTS

Doughnut pendants can be created in a variety of designs. In this project, handmade felt beads are used to provide a contrast with the metal.

You will need:

- 2 x pieces pink felt 0.75 x 1.25 inches (2 x 3.2 cm)
- silver seed beads
- sparkly pink embroidery thread
- beading thread
- medium cotton cord
- large aluminum doughnut
- scissors
- beading needle
- sewing needle

STEP 1

Wrap the felt around a toothpick and use a tiny blob of fabric glue to hold it. Wind the pink embroidery thread around the felt bead. Repeat for the second bead.

STEP 2

Now slide the felt beads onto the cord, placing them almost halfway along the length.

STEP 3

Tie the cord onto the doughnut pendant, positioning the felt beads on the front.

STEP 4

Stitch some silver seed beads to the front of the felt beads.

STEP 5

Attach a regular clasp or tie the cord with a slide knot. You can find instructions on tying knots on many jewelry making Web sites. Then sew clusters of seed beads to the ends for decoration.

Choose a contrasting color for beads and felt to create a dramatic look.

Pendants, such as the Roman **amulet** below, can also be added to chokers.

You will need:

- memory wire choker
- size 8 seed beads
- pendant
- 2 metal feature beads
- flat-nosed pliers

STEP 1

Using pliers, bend one end of the choker wire over to make a loop.

STEP 2

Thread the seed beads on until you have almost reached the center, then add one of the metal feature beads, the pendant, and then the other metal feature bead.

STEP 3

Add the seed beads to the other side of the pendant, leaving one-half inch (1.25 cm) at the end.

STEP 4

Bend the wire over to make another loop, and use the loops to fasten the choker in position.

Experiment with different bead and color combinations.

P E N D A N T S

OTHER NECKLACES

Y ou can combine decorative beads, colorful pendants, and cord to create beautiful necklaces, using a couple of simple methods.

You will need:
- doughnut pendant
- 2 decorative metal beads
- 3.5 feet (1 m) suede ribbon
- 2 flat leather crimps
- 4 crimp beads
- 1 lobster clasp
- round-nosed pliers
- flat-nosed pliers
- scissors

STEP 1

Bring the ends of the suede ribbon together and pass them through the center of the doughnut, leaving a loop of suede behind. Bring the ends back through the loop to knot the pendant.

STEP 2

Thread crimp beads onto each end of the suede, moving them down so that they are just above the doughnut. Secure them with the flat-nosed pliers.

STEP 3

Add a bead to each ribbon. Then add a crimp bead above each one.

Here, knots have been used instead of crimp beads.

STEP 4

Measure the necklace to the right length and trim the excess ribbon. Attach the flat leather crimps to the ends, and then fix the lobster clasp on one side.

Simple rope necklaces decorated with shell buttons are really pretty, and they are very easy to make.

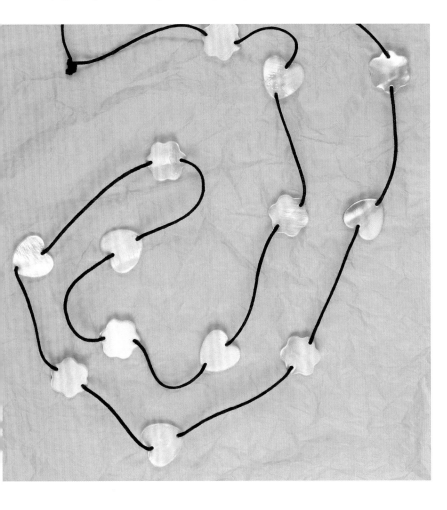

You will need:
- 3.5 feet (1 m) stringing cord
- 14 shell buttons
- scissors

STEP 1

Measure and cut the stringing cord to the right length.

STEP 2

Thread the cord through a hole in a shell button and move it down towards the end. Then thread the cord through the other hole, as shown below.

STEP 3

Continue threading the beads onto the cord alternating the designs. Make sure you leave equal spaces between each bead.

STEP 4

Tie the cord ends in a knot to secure the rope necklace.

For a brightly colored necklace, choose a colorful cord and contrasting beads.

SAFETY PIN BRACELET

Bracelets can be simple pieces of cord, or they can be more ornate and decorated with various charms and beads. This sparkling bracelet is made from safety pins! It is easy to transform these everyday objects into beautiful pieces of jewelry.

You will need:

- 30 x 34mm pink safety pins
- 120 x size 8 pink seed beads
- 60 x pink 4mm cube beads
- 30 x 6mm fire-polished beads
- 2 x 12 inches (30.5 cm) lengths of 1mm clear elastic cord
- 90 x size 6 pink seed beads
- chain-nosed pliers

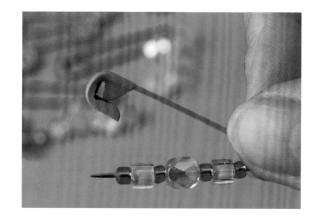

STEP 1

Open a safety pin and thread on the following beads: pink seed bead, pink cube, pink seed bead, fire-polished bead, pink seed bead, pink cube, pink seed bead. Use only the size 8 pink seed beads on the safety pins.

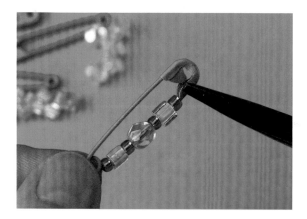

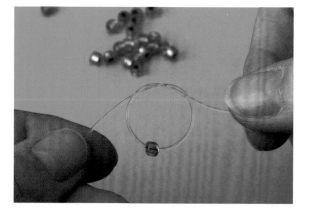

STEP 2

Close the safety pin again, and use the chain-nosed pliers to squash the fastening to seal it shut. Repeat steps 1 and 2 for the remaining safety pins.

STEP 3

Take the elastic cord and tie on a size 6 pink seed bead at a distance of two inches (5 cm) from one end.

STEP 4

Thread on three size 6 pink seed beads, then two safety pins. Make sure you thread through the tops of the safety pins. Now add three more pink seed beads.

STEP 5

Add two more safety pins, this time threading through the bottom end. Repeat steps 4 and 5 until all the safety pins are threaded on the cord.

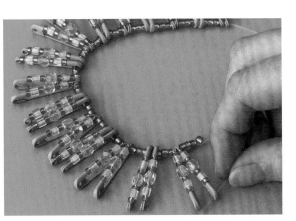

STEP 6

Take the second length of cord and repeat step 3. Then thread it through the bottom of the end safety pin, as shown.

STEP 7

Add three pink seed beads to the thread and go through the end of the next safety pin. Thread through the end of the third safety pin, then add three more pink seed beads. Repeat this pattern all the way around, adding three seed beads after every odd-numbered safety pin.

STEP 8

Remove the stopper bead. Then gather the ends of the elastic together and tie them in a knot, as shown, pulling it tight. Trim the ends, then repeat the process for the second piece of elastic. Trim the ends close to the knots to complete the bracelet.

KNOTTED BRACELETS

Knotted bracelets are simple, but they are very fashionable. Use glass beads because they show up really well against the black lace.

You will need:
- 20 inches (51 cm) black leather lacing
- 1 glass bead
- scissors

STEP 1

Wrap the lacing so that it forms a double loop. Then wrap the right end over the lacing three times, threading the end back through to form a knot.

STEP 2

Thread a glass bead onto the left end. Make a second knot by wrapping the end around the lacing three times, and pulling the end back through.

STEP 3

Trim the excess lacing from the knots. Use a slip knot, so the bracelet can be adjusted easily to fit. You can find instructions on tying knots on many jewelry making Web sites.

Make several bracelets using different colored beads. This one looks very appealing with a blue bead.

These leather bracelets have a beaded charm combined with glass and metal beads.

You will need:
- 4 headpins
- 22 inches (56 cm) black leather lacing
- 4 green glass handmade beads
- 2 silver metal beads
- 1 metal pendant bead
- 12 x 2mm clear, silver-lined seed beads
- 8 x 4mm silver jump rings
- 1 x 8mm silver jump ring
- 2 x 6mm silver end caps
- 1 silver spring fastening
- flat-nosed pliers
- half-round-nosed pliers
- wire cutters
- scissors

STEP 1

Fold the leather lacing in half and cut it at the mid-point. Hold them together and loop them over and through to make a knot near the middle.

STEP 2

Tie a second knot one inch (2.5 cm) from the other, taking the lacing under and through so that the knot faces the opposite way. Put end caps on either end of the double strand.

STEP 3

Attach 2 x 4mm jump rings and then the spring fastening to the end caps.

STEP 4

Take four headpins and thread a seed bead, glass bead, and seed bead onto each. Repeat with two more pins, using metal beads. Use flat-nosed pliers to bend the headpins at right angles, and cut, leaving one-half inch (1.25 cm) of wire above the beads. Bend this into a loop using the round-nosed pliers.

STEP 5

Attach the 8mm jump ring to the metal pendant bead. Divide the threaded headpins into two sets, each containing two glass beads and a metal bead. Thread each set onto a separate jump ring.

STEP 6

Link two jump rings together, then attach one set of beads to each end. Link a jump ring to one end. Attach this to the leather lacing between the two knots. Now add the pendant bead to the final jump ring.

Choose leather lacing to tone with your beads. Brown lacing, for example, works well with pink beads.

KNOTTED BRACELETS

CHARM BRACELETS

Charm bracelets add color to any outfit. Czech beads have polished, faceted surfaces that really catch the light.

You will need:
- 16 x two-inch (5 cm) headpins
- jewelry cable
- 16 x size 8 clear seed beads
- 16 x size 8 turquoise seed beads
- 2 crimp tubes
- lobster clasp and 5mm split ring
- 4 x 5mm silver filigree bell caps
- 2 x 6mm dark turquoise fire-polished beads
- 2 x 6mm clear round glass beads
- 2 x 9mm turquoise matt flower beads
- 2 x 10mm turquoise disk beads
- 2 x 8mm crystal AB fire-polished beads
- 2 x 12mm turquoise AB star beads
- 2 x 10mm crystal AB heart beads
- 2 x 8mm fire-polished turquoise beads
- side cutters
- chain-nosed pliers
- 34 x 3mm silver beads
- 17 x size 5 turquoise triangle beads
- cable snips or scissors
- round-nosed pliers

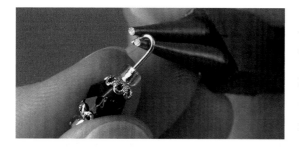

STEP 1

Thread a clear seed bead, filigree bell cap, 6mm fire-polished bead, filigree cap, and another clear seed bead. Trim the headpin, then use round-nosed pliers to make a loop, as shown.

STEP 2

Repeat this for the remaining 15 charms. You will only use the filigree bell caps for the other fire-polished bead. Note that for clear glass beads, turquoise seed beads have been used, and vice versa.

STEP 3

Cut a 12 inch (30.5 cm) length of jewelry cable, and thread a crimp tube and lobster clasp onto one end.

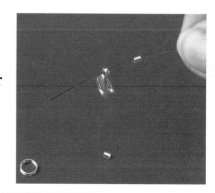

STEP 4

Thread the end of the jewelry cable back through the crimp tube, then flatten it with the pliers. Trim the end of the cable to leave a one-half inch (1.25 cm) tail beyond the crimp tube.

STEP 5

Thread a 3mm silver bead, a triangle bead and another silver bead. Slide the beads down to the clasp end so they cover the trimmed end, then thread on one of the charms.

STEP 6

Repeat step 5 until all the charms are threaded. Now add a silver crimp tube and a split ring. Feed the jewelry cable end back through the crimp bead and two beads.

STEP 7

Squash the crimp tube with chain-nosed pliers, then trim the cable as close to the bead as possible.

FELT BEAD BRACELETS

Felt beads can be combined with wooden beads for an interesting contrast in textures.

STEP 1

Wrap the felt around a toothpick, and use a tiny blob of fabric glue to hold it. Wind the embroidery thread around the felt bead in three sections, as shown. Now sew on seed and bugle beads. Repeat for the remaining felt beads.

STEP 2

Thread the felt beads and wooden spacer beads alternately on the elastic.

STEP 3

Keeping the elastic taut, tie a knot in the end and trim off the excess thread.

STEP 4

Gently pull the elastic so that the knot is tucked inside one of the felt beads.

For a brighter look, use pinks and purples.

Felt beads can also be used to make bangles.

You will need:
- 8 x green felt pieces
  1 x 3 inches (2.5 x 7.5 cm)
- iridescent green seed beads
- iridescent green bugle beads
- copper-colored sparkly
  embroidery thread
- beading thread
- medium cotton cord
- scissors
- beading needle
- sewing needle

STEP 1

Wrap the felt around a toothpick, and use a tiny blob of fabric glue to hold it. Wind the embroidery thread around the felt bead in a criss-cross pattern, as shown. Repeat for the remaining felt beads.

STEP 2

Thread the felt beads onto the cord and knot it securely to make a bangle. As this is a fixed-size bangle, be sure to check the size and add more felt beads if it needs to be larger.

STEP 3

Gently move the knot so that it is tucked inside a felt bead. Then use a needle and embroidery thread to stitch the ends of the felt beads together.

STEP 4

Stitch bugle beads over the stitches to hide them.

STEP 5

Make a string of the seed beads, and wrap them around the bracelet. Stitch it to the cord at intervals to hold it in place.

Light and dark shades of the same color work well for this design.

CHUNKY BEAD BRACELETS

Dramatic, bold bracelets can be created with colorful, chunky beads.

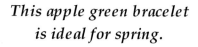

This apple green bracelet is ideal for spring.

You will need:

- 9 mixed fashion beads
- 8 silver metal divider bead rings
- 2 silver drum beads
- 24 inches (61 cm) pink faux leather lacing
- scissors
- darning needle

STEP 1

Thread the darning needle with the lacing, and add a drum bead.

STEP 2

Thread the fashion beads, alternating with the metal rings. Finish by adding the remaining drum bead.

STEP 3

Center the beads along the lacing so that the tails are even. To fasten, tie around the wrist in a bow.

Decorative toggles, or ring and bar clasps, are ideal for heavy bracelets.

STEP 1

Thread a glass bead onto an eye pin. Use flat-nosed pliers to cut the wire one-half inch (1.25 cm) above the bead.

STEP 2

Bend the wire into a loop using the round-nosed pliers. Before you close the loop, thread on another eye pin, then repeat steps 1 and 2 for the remaining beads.

STEP 3

Attach jump rings to the end eye pins. Now attach the decorative ring to one end of the bracelet and the clasp to the other.

This design is particularly attractive if metal beads are used.

RINGS

Seed beads can be used to create a huge range of rings that are relatively easy and cheap to make. They are also perfect for using up leftover beads from other projects.

You will need:
- 3.3 feet (1 m) beading thread
- beading needle
- 60 purple size 11 seed beads
- 15 white size 11 seed beads

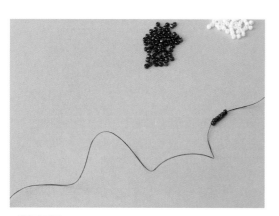

STEP 1

Thread the beading needle and pick up six purple seed beads, sliding them down the thread toward the end. Leave a six-inch (15.25 cm) tail.

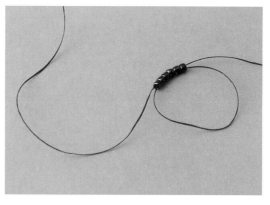

STEP 2

Bring the needle around and stitch through the beads again in the same direction, to create a loop.

STEP 3

Pull the loop to make a little circle, then tie a reef knot—first left over right, then right over left. Pull the knot tight.

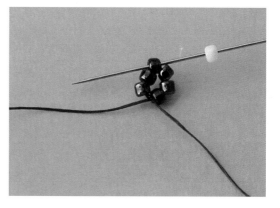

STEP 4

Pick up a white bead and stitch through the third purple bead in the circle. Then push the white bead into the center of the circle.

STEP 5

Pick up two purple beads and one white bead. Stitch through a purple bead on the right-hand side of the daisy, pulling the thread right through.

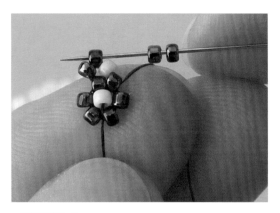

STEP 6

Pick up two purple beads and stitch through the top purple bead of your second daisy, as shown. Pull it through to complete the second flower.

STEP 7

Repeat steps 5 and 6 to make a row of daisies. Now wrap the daisies around your finger to check the length.

STEP 8

To finish your ring, pick up a purple bead on the final daisy and stitch it through two beads of the first daisy.

EARRINGS

Drop earrings are easy to make. By choosing matching colors and materials, you can complete jewelry sets of bracelets, necklaces, and earrings.

You will need:

- 2 orange felt pieces
  1 x 2.5 inches (2.5 x 6.5 cm)
- 4 flat, black spacer beads
- 4 small gold beads
- 2 headpins
- 2 long ball wire
  earring hooks
- gold and yellow seed beads
- gold and yellow bugle beads
- tan embroidery thread
- beading thread
- round-nosed pliers
- flat-nosed pliers
- cutting pliers
- scissors
- beading needle
- sewing needle

STEP 1

Wrap the felt around a toothpick, and use a tiny blob of fabric glue to hold it. Wind the embroidery thread around the felt bead in three bands, as shown. Repeat for the second felt bead. Stitch on a selection of bugle and seed beads as shown.

STEP 2

Take the headpin and thread on the following: small gold bead, flat black spacer, felt bead, flat black spacer, small gold bead.

STEP 3

Cut the excess wire off the headpin, leaving one-half inch (1.25 cm) to bend into a loop. Attach an earring to the loop, then close it with the pliers.

STEP 4

Repeat steps 2 and 3 to make the second earring.

DRAMATIC DROP EARRINGS

Headpins can be used as decorative pieces. Here, they have been used to make long drop earrings.

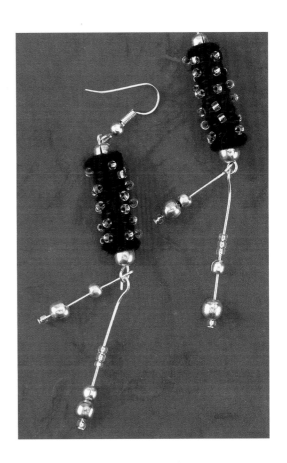

You will need:
- 2 black felt pieces 0.8 x 1.2 inches (2 x 3 cm)
- 8 medium silver beads
- 4 small silver beads
- 4 headpins
- 2 eye pins
- 2 long ball wire earring hooks
- beading thread
- black embroidery thread
- selection of silver seed beads
- round-nosed pliers
- flat-nosed pliers
- cutting pliers
- scissors
- beading needle
- needle

STEP 1

Wrap the felt around a toothpick, and use a tiny blob of fabric glue to hold it. Wind the embroidery thread around the felt bead in four bands, as shown. Repeat for the second bead. Stitch on a selection of bugle and seed beads as shown.

STEP 2

Take an eye pin and thread on a medium silver bead, felt bead, and another medium silver bead.

STEP 3

Cut the eye pin, leaving one-half inch (1.25 cm) of wire. Bend this to create a loop and attach an earring hook.

STEP 4

Thread a headpin with a seed bead, medium silver bead and a small silver bead. Cut to length and create a loop. Repeat for another headpin, this time adding three extra seed beads. Cut to length and create a loop. Attach both headpins to the bottom of the eye pin. The headpins should be different lengths, as shown in the picture.

STEP 5

Repeat the process from start to finish to make the other earring.

HAIR ADORNMENTS

Striking hair decorations are simple to make using beads and wire. You can make hairbands, or twist wire around plain combs, slides or clips to give them a unique look.

You will need:
- 10 feet (3 m) x 24 gauge silver wire
- 160 x 4mm black faceted beads
- 2 black 9 x 6mm oval beads
- black elastic
- wire cutters
- long-nosed pliers
- round-nosed pliers
- ruler
- glue
- toothpick
- scissors

STEP 1

To make a hairband, cut two pieces of wire measuring 54 inches (1.4 m). Hold the pieces together and twist them with your fingers, starting two inches (5 cm) from one end, until you have twisted one-half inch (1.25 cm).

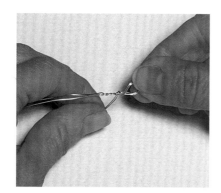

STEP 2

Take the two-inch (5 cm) tails and loop them around the round-nosed pliers. Wrap the ends around the twisted section. Trim the excess with the wire cutters.

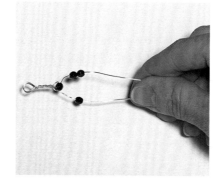

STEP 3

Take a faceted bead. Holding the ends of the wire apart, thread the top wire down and the bottom wire up. Push the bead to the end of the wires, near the loop. Now thread two beads on the top wire, and one on the bottom.

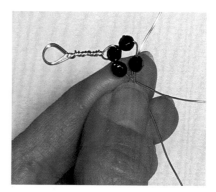

STEP 4

Thread the bottom wire up through the second top bead, bending it around to create a cluster.

STEP 5

Measure two inches (5 cm) along the wire, then thread four beads onto the bottom wire. Pull it up, around, and back through the first bead to create another cluster. Repeat this with the top wire.

STEP 6

Measure two inches (5 cm) down the wire, then repeat steps 3 and 4 to create another central bead cluster, then repeat step 5 to create two more clusters, as shown.

STEP 7

Repeat steps 3, 4, and 5 until the hairband is complete.

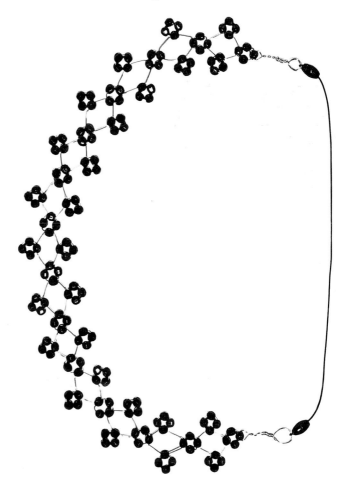

STEP 8

Tie on a piece of elastic (be sure to check the length first). Knot it, then add a dot of glue using the toothpick. Thread on an oval bead, pulling it down to the knot. Pull through the elastic tail then slide the bead over the glued knot. Thread on the second oval bead, then knot and glue the elastic, sliding the bead over the knot to complete the band.

OTHER DECORATIVE ITEMS

Now that you have mastered the basics of jewelry making, try using the techniques to decorate other items. You can decorate almost any everyday item with beads to create unusual gifts and feature pieces.

ABSTRACT DECORATION

This hanging decoration was put together by suspending lengths of clear string threaded with beads and polished glass from a piece of driftwood. Wrapping the glass in fine wire adds an extra decorative touch.

GLASS AND WIRE

You can string beads on colorful wire, then wrap them around clear glass. Here, they are decorating a vase, but you could also put them on drinking glasses, perfume bottles, or bath oils to make unique gifts. Vary the combinations of beads and gauges of wire for different effects.

BEADED CURTAIN

Thread beads onto clear string to make a bead curtain. Colored glass or plastic beads will look really pretty hung against a window so that they sparkle in the sunlight.

PHONE CHARMS AND KEYCHAINS

You can create small charms for your cellular phone by threading beads onto cord or leather ribbons. These are cheap and simple to make, so you can change them whenever you like! Use the techniques used to make the safety pin charm bracelet on page 30 to create a bead keychain.

GIFT WRAP

Beads can also be used to jazz up gift wrapping. Pick beads in a color to tone with the wrapping paper, and fasten to a bow for a really classy look.

GLOSSARY

abstract Colors and shapes used to create an effect, rather than represent reality

amulet A charm, usually worn around the neck or carried in a pouch, believed by some people to ward off evil

Art Deco Art style, popular in the 1920s and 1930s, famous for its geometric shapes

Art Nouveau Art style, popular at the turn of the 20th century, famous for its intricate form and flowing curves

cameo A carving of a profile of someone against a different color background

charm A small decorative piece, often hanging from a bracelet

contrast Opposing colors or forms placed close to each other for intense effect

depth A richness of color that creates the idea of dimension

enamel A highly colorful finish on metal produced by heating special powdered glass at high temperatures

facet Flat polished surface cut onto a bead or stone

filigree Delicate and intricate twisted wirework, often in gold or silver

fire-polished A method used to make beads smooth and shiny, also called Czech beads

geometric A design with a regular pattern and shape.

metal oxide A substance formed from a combination of oxygen and metal

ocher One of the earliest forms of pigment, made from earth in colors from light yellow, to red, and brown

pigment A substance used to color or paint

spacer beads Small beads, usually not the focal point of a piece; a number of spacer beads can be used to lead to a larger object on the piece

symbol An object, mark, or character used to represent something; for example, a cross is worn by Christians

texture How an object feels to the touch

threading Joining a series of beads by running a thread, cord, or ribbon through them

INDEX